I'm a NEUTRINO

Tiny Particles in a Big Universe

Dr. Eve M. Vavagiakis

illustrated by **Ilze Lemesis**

≡ mit Kids Press

Hi! I'm a neutrino, and I am so small

that matter to me barely matters at all.

I am a particle, like electrons and light.

I can pass through you without stopping my flight!

I'm electrically neutral; I don't have a charge.

And with my small mass, I don't feel very large.

Compared to you? When I am at rest
I'm 10^{38} (10 to the 38th power) lighter, at best!

I am a fermion that can hardly be traced.
I come in flavors, but not ones you can taste.

Electron, muon, and tau are the flavors I crave.
The flavor I have determines how I'll behave.

If I don't like my flavor? I can change on a dime.

That's called flavor oscillation. Like lemon to lime.

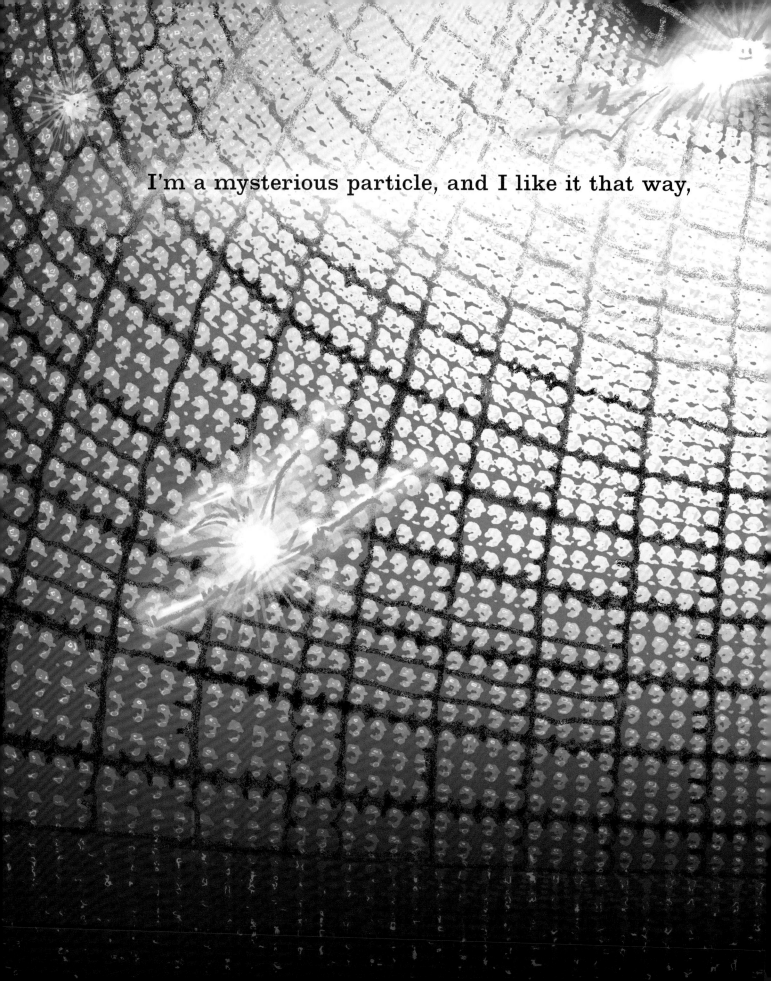

I'm a mysterious particle, and I like it that way,

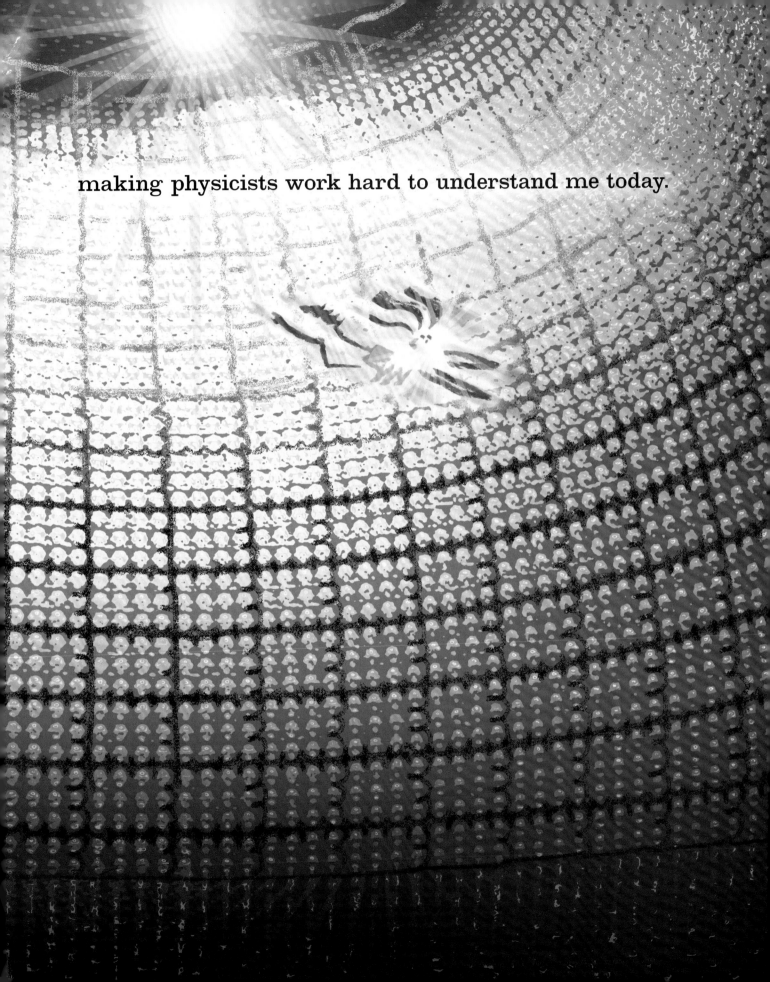

making physicists work hard to understand me today.

They still don't know my mass!
Can you believe that it's true?

Who will find out? Could it one day be you?

My friends and I travel from more than one place.

We come from the sun, or the earth, or from space.

Maybe one day you will learn more of our traits

as you study how we travel and oscillate.

Even though my friends and I are so small,
we can teach you the biggest things of all.

We've worked together since the beginning, in fact,

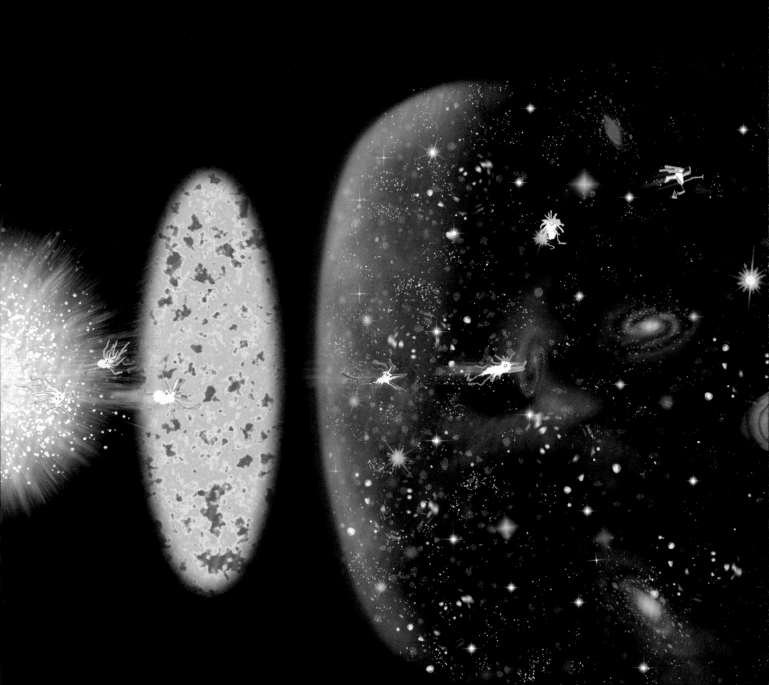

so long that the whole universe felt our impact.

If you look through the right telescope, up into space,

you'll find our imprint on galaxies.

We're all over the place!

So although I am small, and secretive, too,
I matter to the universe, and I matter to you.

Know Your Neutrinos

Neutrinos are tiny particles, but the universe is filled with them. You can't see neutrinos, so our cheeky neutrino friends in this book are a fun but unrealistic artist's rendition. Here you see our home galaxy, the Milky Way, along with a neutrino. It would be one of trillions upon trillions in our galaxy.

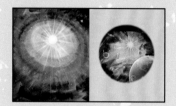

Objects are made of matter, which has mass and takes up space. This image shows a protoplanetary disk, which is made of matter. It surrounds a newborn star and is similar to a nursery where planets like our own Earth are born. Neutrinos don't interact much with this kind of matter.

Electrons and photons (also known as light, like the kind shining from our own sun) are examples of particles. Particles are the fundamental building blocks of all of the matter in our universe. Neutrinos are particles, too, but don't interact with other particles the way electrons or photons do.

Neutrinos really do fly right through us—trillions every second! They can do this because they are very small and very light and don't interact with the particles in our body the way other particles do. Neutrinos only interact with other particles through the force of gravity and through the weak force, which acts on tiny distances, smaller than the size of an atom.

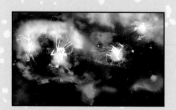

Neutrinos can't interact through the electromagnetic force, which is how we interact with most matter around us. We can feel pushes and pulls based on positive or negative electric charges. Neutrinos have no charge, so they're free to pass through everything. Their mass is so small that about a billion billion billion billion (that's 1 with 36 zeros after it) neutrinos equal the weight of a lemon. To add up to as much as we weigh, you'd need about a hundred billion billion billion billion neutrinos! That's a 1 with 38 zeros after it, or 10^{38}.

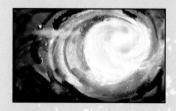

A neutrino is a type of particle called a fermion, which means it acts in a certain predictable way. There are three known kinds of neutrinos: electron neutrinos, muon neutrinos, and tau neutrinos. These are known as neutrino "flavors."

The left page shows an artist's imagining of electron, muon, and tau neutrinos. As a neutrino zooms through space, it changes its flavor over and over again as it travels. This flavor oscillation means that if you start with an electron neutrino, you might soon end up with a muon or tau neutrino.

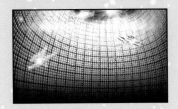

Neutrino oscillation was discovered in 1998. The 2015 Nobel Prize in Physics was given to Arthur B. McDonald and Takaaki Kajita for their work on the Sudbury Neutrino Observatory and Super-Kamiokande (Super-K) experiments, which proved that neutrinos have mass and change their flavors as they travel. Here, you see the inside of the Super-K detector, with more than 11,000 sensitive photomultipliers that can pick up tiny signals when neutrinos interact with the matter inside the detector.

It's really hard to measure such tiny masses (or weights, on Earth). Physicists have been learning more about the total mass of the three neutrino flavors and what each might weigh individually. They have defined limits on these masses, but don't know exactly what each neutrino weighs. Someone will find out eventually . . . Will it be you?

Physicists can learn about the sum of the neutrino masses in different ways, depending on where the neutrinos they're studying are coming from. We can look at neutrinos from our sun, from Earth's atmosphere, from nuclear reactors and particle accelerators, and indirectly by studying the night sky up in space.

Here we can see some neutrinos flying along in a beam, which particle physicists can create to study how neutrinos behave as they travel long distances.

Scientists can study neutrinos here on Earth by using particle accelerators to create beams of neutrinos. If the neutrinos travel a short distance, scientists can study them before they change flavors. If they travel very far away, we can learn about how they oscillate. Both kinds of experiments, such as those at the Fermi National Accelerator Laboratory (Fermilab), can teach us a lot about these elusive particles.

As small and mysterious as they are, neutrinos actually had an impact on how the whole universe evolved! By studying the largest things in the universe, such as clusters of galaxies like our own Milky Way, we can learn things about the neutrinos in our universe, too.

These pages depict the history of the universe with time running from left to right. Our universe can be described as starting with the Big Bang 13.8 billion years ago. Right afterward, neutrinos were born. The first photons we can see today were emitted about 380,000 years after the Big Bang. After that, the night sky as we know it evolved, with stars, galaxies, and planets being formed.

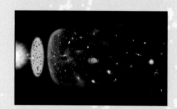

These pages show the Atacama Cosmology Telescope taking special photos of the night sky to look at the first photons emitted after the Big Bang. This is called the cosmic microwave background. In the patterns of this light, you can learn about large-scale structure, the way galaxies and galaxy clusters are clumping in our universe (as illustrated by the blue webby pattern shown here). And by learning about how the galaxy clusters move around, you can learn about those ancient neutrinos that zoomed around space billions of years ago.

Even though we can't see neutrinos as they fly through everything around us, we know that they helped make the universe into what it is today. Small things can make a really big difference in our world. Thanks, neutrinos.

FOR FURTHER EXPLORATION

Check out the websites below to learn more about the science in this book.

On the Atacama Cosmology Telescope: https://act.princeton.edu/

On the history of our universe: https://spaceplace.nasa.gov/big-bang/en/

On neutrinos: https://neutrinos.fnal.gov/

On particle accelerators at Fermilab: https://www.fnal.gov/pub/science/particle-accelerators/

On the Super-Kamiokande experiment: http://www-sk.icrr.u-tokyo.ac.jp/sk/index-e.html

Text copyright © 2022 by Eve M. Vavagiakis
Illustrations copyright © 2022 by Ilze Lemesis

The MIT Press, the ☰ mit Kids Press colophon, and MIT Kids Press are trademarks of The MIT Press,
a department of the Massachusetts Institute of Technology, and used under license from The MIT Press.
The colophon and MIT Kids Press are registered in the US Patent and Trademark Office.

First edition 2022

Library of Congress Catalog Card Number 2021946946
ISBN 978-1-5362-2207-4

21 22 23 24 25 26 CCP 10 9 8 7 6 5 4 3 2 1

Printed in Shenzhen, Guangdong, China

This book was typeset in Egyptienne Extended.
The illustrations were created digitally.

MIT Kids Press
an imprint of Candlewick Press
99 Dover Street
Somerville, Massachusetts 02144

mitkidspress.com
candlewick.com